MUSICAL
INSTRUMENTS
OF THE WORLD

Percussion

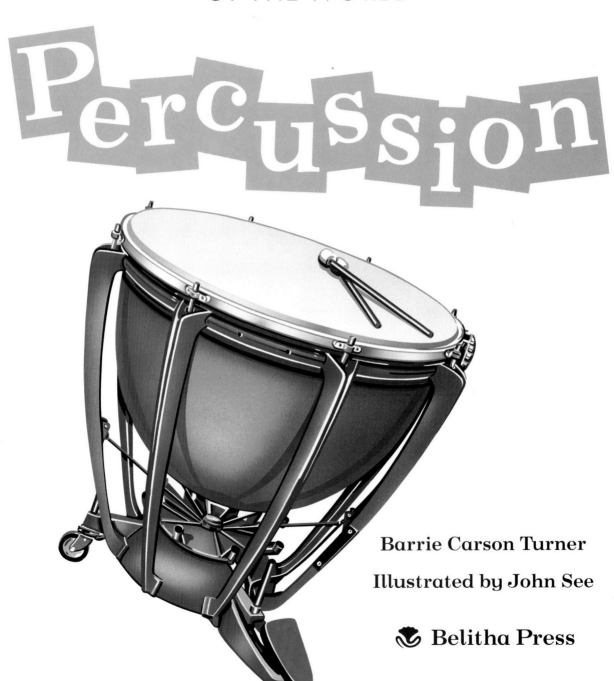

Barrie Carson Turner

Illustrated by John See

Belitha Press

First published in the UK in 1998 by
Belitha Press Limited
London House, Great Eastern Wharf,
Parkgate Road, London SW11 4NQ

Editor: Claire Edwards
Series designer: Simeen Karim
Picture researcher: Juliet Duff
Educational consultant: Celia Pardaens

ISBN 1 85561 790 0

Printed in Hong Kong / China

British Library Cataloguing in Publication Data
for this book is available from the British Library.

9 8 7 6 5 4 3 2 1

Picture acknowledgements: Axiom Photographic Agency: 27 James Morris;
The Hutchison Library: 4-5 Liba Taylor; Impact Photos: 22 Bruce Stephens;
Panos Pictures: 9 David Reed, 10-11 Guy Mansfield, 16-17 Sean Sprague;
Performing Arts Library: 13 Fritz Curzon, 14, 16 Clive Barda, 20-21 Steve Gillett,
28-29 Jane Mont Mitchell; Redferns: 6, 7, 12, 23, 26 Odile Noel, 8 Brigitte Engl,
24-25 David Redfern; Travel Link: 15 Brenda Kean; John Walmsley: 19.

Contents

Musical

Musical instruments are played in every country of the world. There are many thousands of different instruments of all shapes and sizes. They are often grouped into four families: strings, brass, percussion and woodwind.

Percussion instruments are struck (hit), shaken or scraped to make their sound. Brass and woodwind instruments are blown to make their sound. String instruments sound when their strings vibrate.

instruments

This book is about the percussion family. Some of the instruments are quite unusual, and they certainly make some strange sounds. Here you will find crashing cymbals, booming gongs, clicking castanets, talking drums and jingling tambourines.

We have chosen 19 percussion instruments from around the world for this book. There is a picture of each instrument, and a photograph of a performer playing it. On pages 30 and 31 you will find a list of useful words to help you understand more about music.

Timpani

Timpani are large drums that are part of an orchestra. Most orchestras have three or four timpani. The timpani player (called a timpanist) presses a pedal at the bottom of the drum to change the pitch (make the notes higher or lower). The top of the drum is called the head or the skin. The body is called the bowl. Timpani are also called kettledrums.

Timpanists strike the top of the drums with drumsticks. Some drumsticks have soft felt ends, others have hard wooden ends.

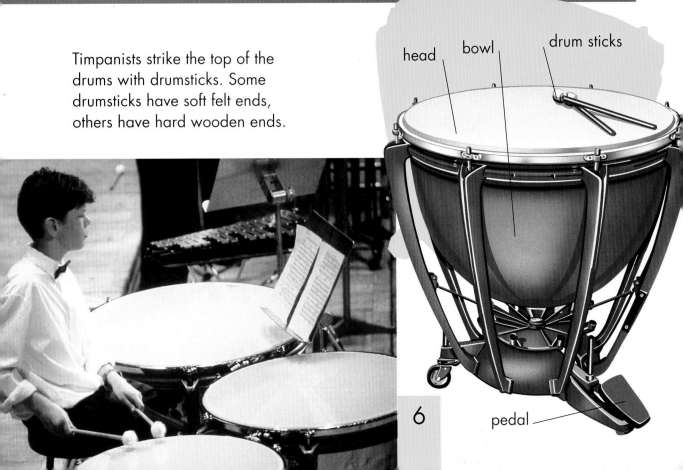

head

bowl

drum sticks

pedal

Xylophone

The wooden notes of a xylophone (zy-low-fone) are called bars. They rest on pads or cords, so that they ring clearly when they are struck. Small xylophones have a hollow wooden box underneath, others have a tube hanging below each bar. The box and the tubes make the sound louder.

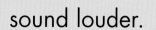

metal tubes (resonators)

bars

beaters

The xylophone is played with wooden sticks called beaters. Each beater has a round plastic or rubber head.

Gong

mallet

bent-back edge

boss

stand

The gong is made from a large metal plate. In the middle there is a raised part called the boss. When this is struck it makes the best sound. The gong is so big it hangs on a stand. It is played with a wooden stick called a mallet, which has a soft felt head.

When the gong is struck hard it makes a loud booming sound, which lasts a long time. Struck softly it sounds mysterious.

Sansa

The sansa is from Africa. Its base is made from a wooden board or box, or a gourd (like a small pumpkin). On top of this, thin strips of iron are held in place by iron rods. Each strip sounds a different note. The long strips make the lowest sounds. The shorter strips make higher sounds.

iron tongue

board

iron rod

The player holds the sansa in both hands while he plucks the iron strips with his thumbs. The sansa is also called the mbira, or thumb piano.

9

Steel drums

The steel drums were invented about 60 years ago by Caribbean islanders. They discovered that the tops of large oil drums can make musical notes. Steel drums are played in sets.

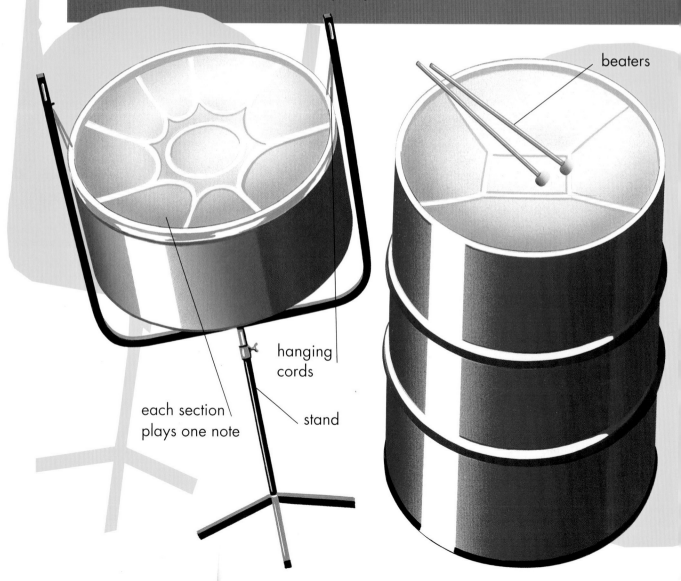

beaters

hanging
cords

each section
plays one note

stand

Players hit the top of the drums with short sticks, called beaters. Steel drums make a bright, tinny sound, almost like bells.

The largest drums play low notes. The highest-sounding drum, which plays the tune, is called the ping-pong. To make steel drums, drum makers first saw off the bottom of an oil drum. Then the top is beaten into a saucer shape. Next, the drum maker divides the top into sections by making deep grooves in the metal. Each section is tapped and shaped until it sounds the correct note.

Cymbals

Cymbals have been played for thousands of years. They are thin and round, with a raised area in the middle. Cymbals have been made from many kinds of metal, even from gold. The tiniest cymbals are less than 5 centimetres across, and are played between the fingers.

bronze metal

leather holding strap

raised area

Players hold a cymbal in each hand. They can clash them together loudly, or rub them together quietly.

Scraper

Any instrument that is scraped with a stick to make its sound is called a scraper. Scrapers are often made from bark, or from a fruit called a gourd (like a small pumpkin). If the surface of the scraper is already rough, it is ready for scraping. A smooth surface must have ridges cut into it.

rough surface

stick

Musicians scrape the instrument firmly to make a hard rasping sound. In an orchestra scrapers are usually made of wood.

Glockenspiel

The glockenspiel (glock-en-shpeel) has metal notes, called bars. It is played with two beaters, with round, hard ends. In an orchestra it rests on a table or on a stand. Glockenspiels are popular in marching bands. They are turned upright so the notes face the player. Glockenspiel is a German word meaning play of bells.

Players strike the bars in the middle to make the best sound. The sound of the glockenspiel is high and bell like.

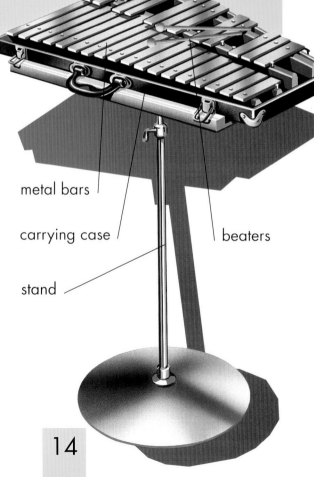

metal bars

carrying case

stand

beaters

Castanets

Castanets are played in pairs. They are held in the hand and clicked together. The instruments are wooden, and shaped like a shell. They are hollowed out in the centre, which makes the click sound louder. In Spain dancers hold a pair of castanets in each hand, clicking them in time to their dance movements.

hollowed-out centre

thick cord

Dancers hold castanets by looping a cord round the thumb. They hold higher-sounding smaller castanets in the right hand, and lower-sounding larger ones in the left hand.

Marimba

The marimba comes from Africa, where it is very popular in many areas. It has wooden notes, called bars, and is played with two sticks called beaters. If you play the notes from left to right the sounds become higher as the bars get smaller.

The marimba is played in many parts of the world. Some very large marimbas are played by several musicians at once.

6

Large marimbas rest on a stand. Smaller ones hang round the player's neck. Some instruments have hollowed out gourds (a pear-shaped fruit) beneath the notes. These make the sound louder and more rounded. In an orchestra a marimba looks like a large xylophone, but its notes are lower.

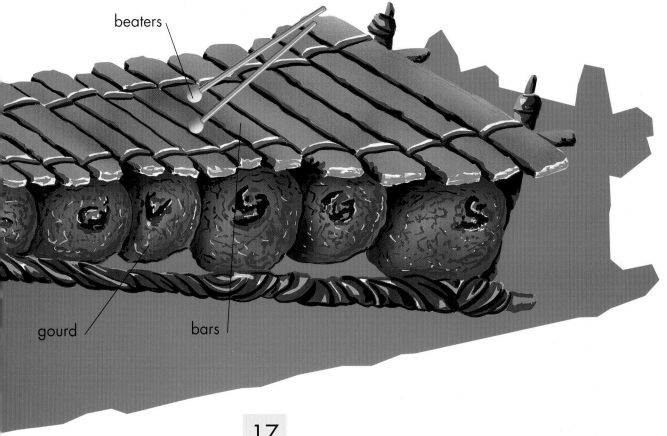

beaters

gourd

bars

Tubular bells

Tubular bells are metal tubes that sound like bells. They hang on a metal frame, with the longest tubes on the left. The longer tubes make low sounds. The shorter tubes make high sounds. Each bell hangs from a string, so that it can vibrate freely when it is struck.

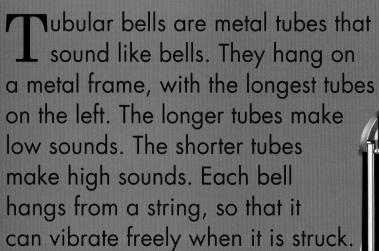

mallet

The player taps the tubes near the top with a small wooden hammer called a mallet.

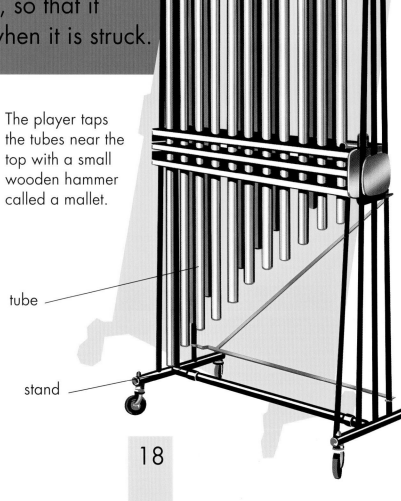

tube

stand

Claves

smooth
surface

The claves are two solid, tube-shaped sticks. The sticks are made from hard, smooth wood, so that they make a bright, crisp click. Claves are also called percussion sticks. They were first played in Cuba. They are often used in South American dance music. They tap out important rhythms and help to keep the beat.

rounded stick

The player holds one of the claves lightly in the palm of one hand and taps it with the other clave.

Rattles

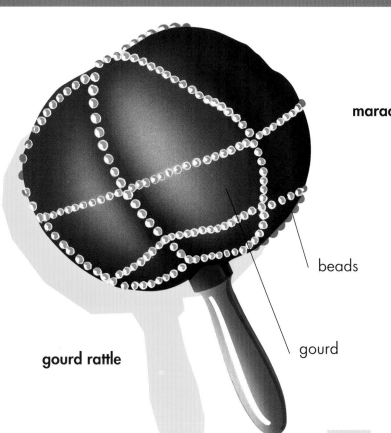

Rattles have been played for thousands of years. They are played in many types of music around the world. Maracas are hollow wooden rattles with pellets inside. They are often used in South American dance music.

maracas

hollow
wooden body

gourd rattle

beads

gourd

sleigh bells

bell

Sleigh bells are another kind of rattle. They are tiny metal bells tied to a strap or stick. Their jingly sound reminds us of Christmas. The gourd rattle is made from a pear-shaped fruit called a gourd. The fruit is dried until the seeds inside rattle when it is shaken. Sometimes the gourd is hollowed out and filled with other objects, such as stones or small shells.

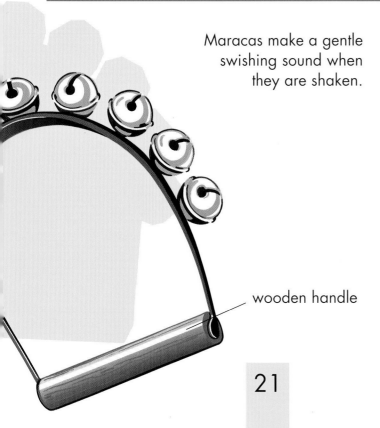

Maracas make a gentle swishing sound when they are shaken.

wooden handle

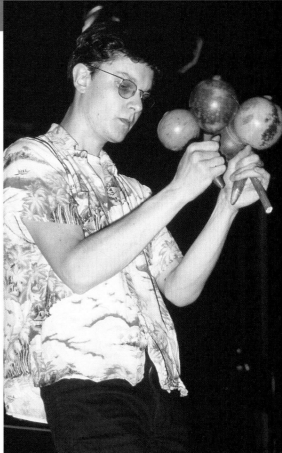

Tambourine

The tambourine looks like a small drum, with small metal discs cut into the side. The discs are called jingles and are like tiny cymbals. When a player taps the tambourine, the discs make a jingling sound. The top of the tambourine is called the skin, and the wooden side is called the frame.

skin

Players hold the tambourine in one hand and strike it with the other. Sometimes they shake it in the air.

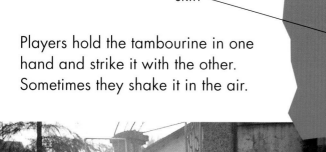

frame

jingles

22

Tabla

The tabla is the name given to two drums from India. They often accompany a string instrument called the sitar. The top of the drum is called the head or skin. In the centre of each skin, players smear a special black paste. This is called tuning paste, and it helps to make the sound clear and crisp. The drums rest on the floor on thick padded rings.

tuning paste

skin

Drummers sit cross-legged on the floor.
They play with their fingertips and wrists.
The larger drum plays the lower sounds.

23

Drum kit

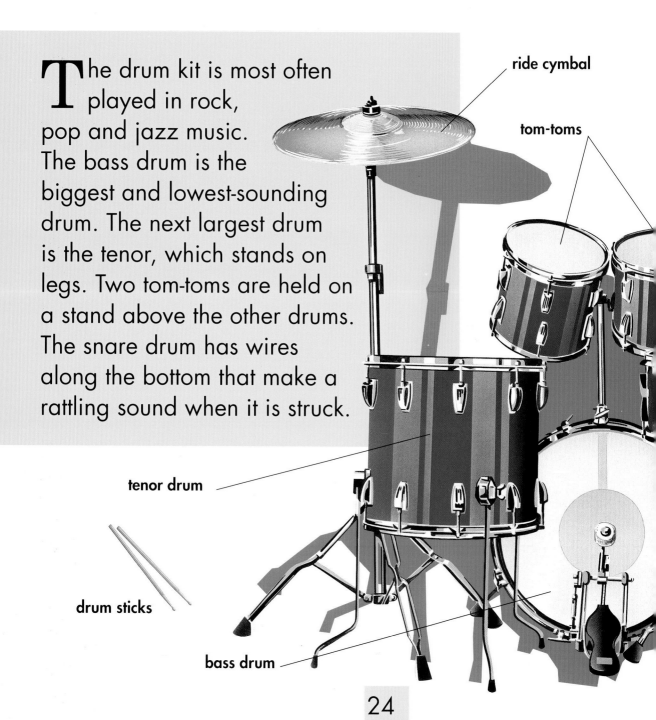

The drum kit is most often played in rock, pop and jazz music. The bass drum is the biggest and lowest-sounding drum. The next largest drum is the tenor, which stands on legs. Two tom-toms are held on a stand above the other drums. The snare drum has wires along the bottom that make a rattling sound when it is struck.

ride cymbal

tom-toms

tenor drum

drum sticks

bass drum

There are cymbals in a drum kit too. The biggest is the ride cymbal, which is played softly. The hi-hat is two cymbals in one, clashed together by a foot pedal. The crash cymbal is named after the loud sound it makes.

crash cymbal

snare drum

hi-hat

Almost every band has a drummer. People often dance to pop music, and the drum kit is important because it plays the beat.

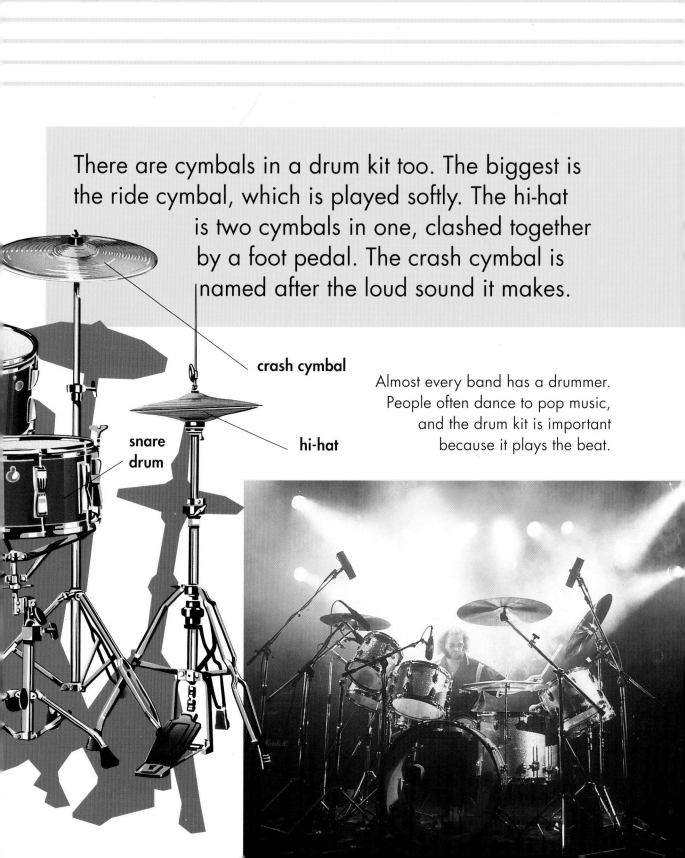

Triangle

The triangle is a very ancient instrument. It is made from a thin steel bar bent into a triangle shape with one corner left open. It is held by a leather strap or string. Sometimes it hangs from a music stand. It is played with a short metal rod called a beater, and makes a high tinkling sound.

If a player taps the triangle it makes a quiet sound. For loud sounds the beater is moved quickly from side to side.

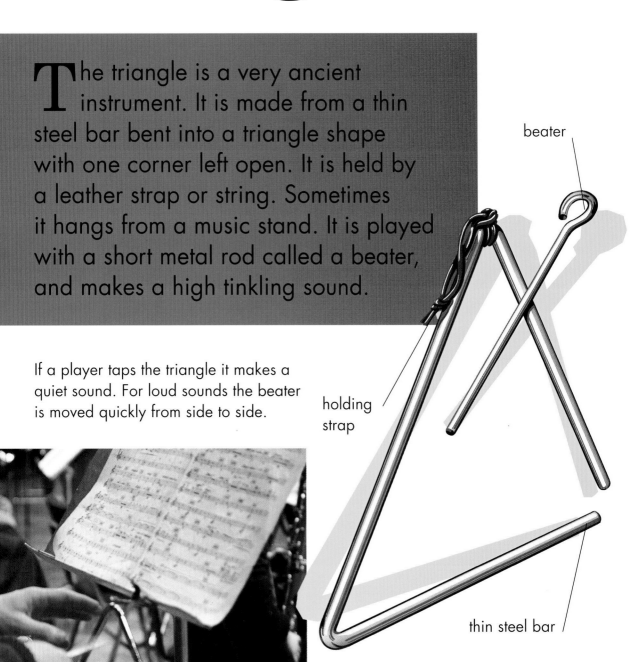

beater

holding strap

thin steel bar

26

Talking drum

skin

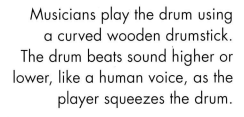

Talking drums are played in many parts of Africa. Players hold the drum under one arm and squeeze the sides in and out. This pulls the strings, which stretches the skin at the top. As the skin gets tighter the pitch of the drum becomes higher.

string

drumstick

Musicians play the drum using a curved wooden drumstick. The drum beats sound higher or lower, like a human voice, as the player squeezes the drum.

Bonang

The bonang comes from Indonesia. It is a large instrument made up of a set of gongs. Each gong is polished and shaped like a cooking pot with deep sides. The high raised area in the centre is called the boss. Striking the boss makes the best sound.

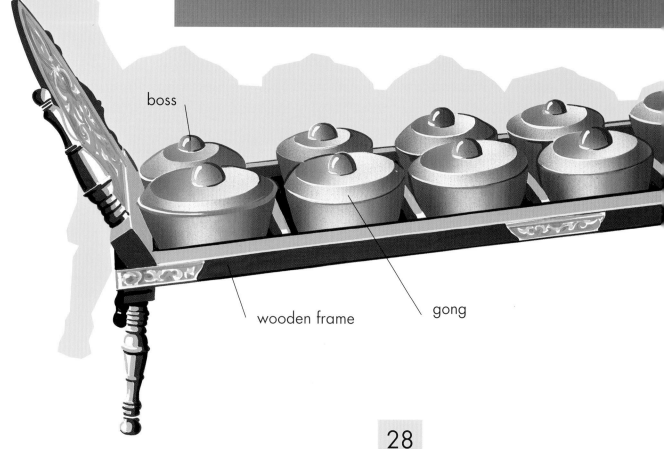

boss

wooden frame

gong

The gongs rest on cords so that they can vibrate freely. The cords are fastened to a carved wooden frame. Each gong sounds a different note. The bonang is played in the gamelan orchestra. It is used to accompany the tune.

Musicians strike the gongs with soft-ended sticks called beaters. The gongs make a soft bell-like sound.

Words to

accompany To play music alongside a singer or another musician who is playing the tune.

bars The notes on some percussion instruments, such as the xylophone. The bars are struck with beaters to make the sound.

beat The steady pulse of the music.

beaters Sticks of wood or wire used to hit or strike some instruments. The ends may be made of felt or rubber.

boss The raised area in the centre of a gong.

bowl The round, deep body of a drum.

cord A thin piece of rope, or twisted pieces of string or silk.

family (of instruments) Instruments that are similar to each other.

frame A narrow band of wood on a small drum. The skin is stretched over the frame.

gamelan orchestra An orchestra from Indonesia. Most of the instruments in a gamelan are percussion instruments.

head The part of a drum that is struck. It is also called the skin.

jazz A kind of pop music. In jazz, musicians often make up the music at the same time as they play it.

mallet A tiny wooden hammer used to play some instruments. It usually has a soft felt head.

marching band A group of musicians who play military (soldiers') music as they march along.

musician Someone who plays an instrument or sings.

remember

oil drum A large, round, metal container, in which oil is stored.

orchestra A large group of musicians playing together.

pedal Any part of an instrument worked by the foot.

pellets Tiny balls of metal or other material inside a rattle.

performer Someone who plays or sings to other people.

pitch How high or low a sound is.

rattle An instrument that is shaken to make its sound.

resonator A tube, box, or gourd placed below the notes on a xylophone or marimba. They make the sound of the instrument louder and more rounded.

rhythm A rhythm is made by the beat of the music, and by how long and short the notes are.

rock A type of pop music, which often has a strong beat.

scraper Any instrument that is scraped to make its sound.

sets Different sizes of the same instrument.

sitar One of the most important string instruments in India.

skin The part of a drum that is struck. It is also called the head.

strike To play an instrument by hitting it.

vibrate To move up and down very quickly. When a string is bowed it vibrates.

Index